BOOKWORMS

Creepy Crawlers

Termites

Jack K. Patterson

Cavendish Square
New York

Published in 2019 by Cavendish Square Publishing, LLC
243 5th Avenue, Suite 136, New York, NY 10016

First Edition

Library of Congress Cataloging-in-Publication Data

Names: Patterson, Jack K., 1988- author.
Title: Termites / Jack K. Patterson.
Description: First edition. | New York : Cavendish Square, 2019. | Series: Creepy crawlers |
Audience: Grades K-3. | Includes bibliographical references and index.
Identifiers: LCCN 2018024815 (print) | LCCN 2018025900 (ebook) | ISBN 9781502642882 (ebook) |
ISBN 9781502642707 (library bound) | ISBN 9781502642868 (pbk.) | ISBN 9781502642875 (6 pack)
Subjects: LCSH: Termites--Juvenile literature.
Classification: LCC QL529 (ebook) | LCC QL529 .P38 2019 (print) | DDC 595.7/36--dc23
LC record available at https://lccn.loc.gov/2018024815

Editorial Director: David McNamara
Editor: Kristen Susienka
Copy Editor: Nathan Heidelberger
Associate Art Director: Alan Sliwinski
Designer: Megan Metté
Production Coordinator: Karol Szymczuk
Photo Research: J8 Media

The photographs in this book are used by permission and through the courtesy of: Cover, Romolo Tavani/Shutterstock.com; p. 5 Sanjay Acharya, Own work/File: Isoptera.jpg/Wikimedia Commons/CCA-SA 4.0 International; p. 7, 15 Piotr Naskrecki/Minden Pictures/Getty Images; p.9 Forestry and Forest Products, CSIRO/ File: CSIRO ScienceImage 1202 A Reproductive Termite.jpg/Wikimedia Commons/CCA 3.0 Unported; p. 11 Kevin Schafer/Photolibrary/Getty Images; p. 13 Beverly Joubert/National Geographic/Getty Images; p. 17 Mrs. Sucharut Chounyoo/Shutterstock.com; p. 19 Panupon Eurawong/Shutterstock.com; p. 21 Bryan Mullennix/The Image Bank/Getty Images.

Printed in the United States of America

Contents

Termites are creepy bugs!

They have six legs and short bodies.

Termites start life inside an egg.

The egg **hatches**.

Hatched termites are called **larvae**.

Larvae turn into young termites.

They are called **nymphs**.

Nymphs **shed** their skin
to grow.

9

A termite lives in a group.

The group is called a colony.

A termite colony is very big.

Millions of termites can live in one colony.

Every termite has a job.

Some termites build homes.

Other termites are fighters.

Others start new colonies.

15

Each termite colony has a queen.

The queen can live for many years.

Everyone wants to **protect** the queen.

Termites eat all the time.

They like to eat wood.

Termites can live in trees
or dirt.

Sometimes they live in
human homes.

Have you ever seen
a termite?

New Words

hatches (HATCH-ez) When an animal or insect leaves an egg.

larvae (LAR-vay) Termites that have hatched from an egg

nymphs (NIMFS) Termites that are no longer newborns but are not yet adults.

protect (pro-TEKT) To keep safe.

shed (SHED) To get rid of an outer layer of skin.

Index

About the Author

Jack K. Patterson lives in Boston, Massachusetts. He enjoys gardening, bird watching, and exploring the outdoors. He is an insect enthusiast who has his own bug collection. He enjoys learning about the world around him.

About BOOKWORMS

Bookworms help independent readers gain reading confidence through high-frequency words, simple sentences, and strong picture/text support. Each book explores a concept that helps children relate what they read to the world they live in.